UNIVERSITY HIGH SCHOOL LIBRARY
UNIVERSITY OF WYOMING

WITHDRAWN

DATE DUE	
FEB 02 1987	NOV 04 1997
JUN 21 1988	
MAY 17 1989	MAY 30 1999
AUG 13 1991	OCT 13 2006
	DEC 13 2010
NOV 14 1991	
DEC 30 1991	
JUL 15 1993	
AUG 16 1993	
OCT 07 1993	
DEC 11 1993	
MAY 31 1994	
JAN 4 1995	
DEC 28 1995	
DEC 30 1996	
MAR 13 1998	

HIGHSMITH 45-220

BEFORE
THE INDIANS

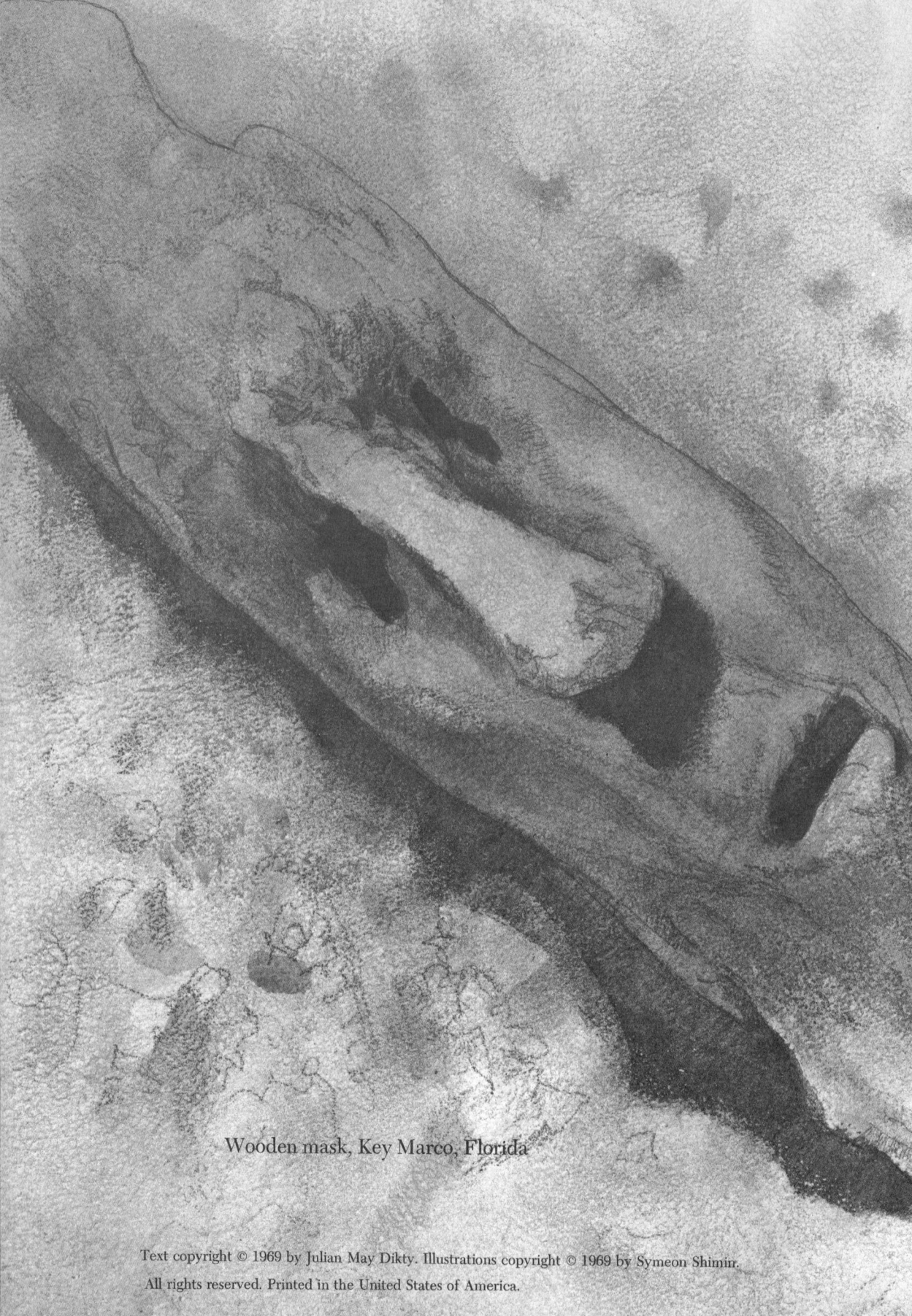

Wooden mask, Key Marco, Florida

Text copyright © 1969 by Julian May Dikty. Illustrations copyright © 1969 by Symeon Shimin.
All rights reserved. Printed in the United States of America.

BEFORE THE INDIANS

JULIAN MAY
illustrations by
SYMEON SHIMIN

Holiday House • New York

Explorers from Europe came to North America nearly 500 years ago. They found people living in the New World, and called them Indians. The Indians did not all live in the same way. Some of them lived in villages and planted crops.

Jacques Cartier visiting an Indian village on the St. Lawrence River about 1535

Other Indians got most of their food through hunting, or gathering wild plants. Settlers soon discovered that there were many different kinds of Indians with different languages, different clothing, different religions, and different art.

Coronado meets primitive desert people about 1540.

And there were mysteries, too. In the river valleys of the East and Midwest, settlers found mounds of earth built by men. The Indians said that the mounds had been made by "old people"—their ancestors who lived there long before the Indians.

Mound of Ohio River Valley

Out in the dry Southwest, settlers found great ruined houses built against cliffs. The Navajo Indians said that they did not make the cliff dwellings. They said the "old enemy," or Anasazi, people had built them long ago.

These ruins are now part of Mesa Verde National Park, in Colorado.

Through the years, scientists have discovered many traces of people who lived in North America before the Indians, who are descended from them. The science of studying vanished people is called archaeology.

Remains of ancient people and the things they made are often found buried in the earth.

It is not easy to study the ancient people who lived before the Indians. They left no writings behind. Archaeologists can study only the things the people made— and sometimes the bones of the people themselves.

These things last for hundreds or even thousands of years, because they do not rot away.

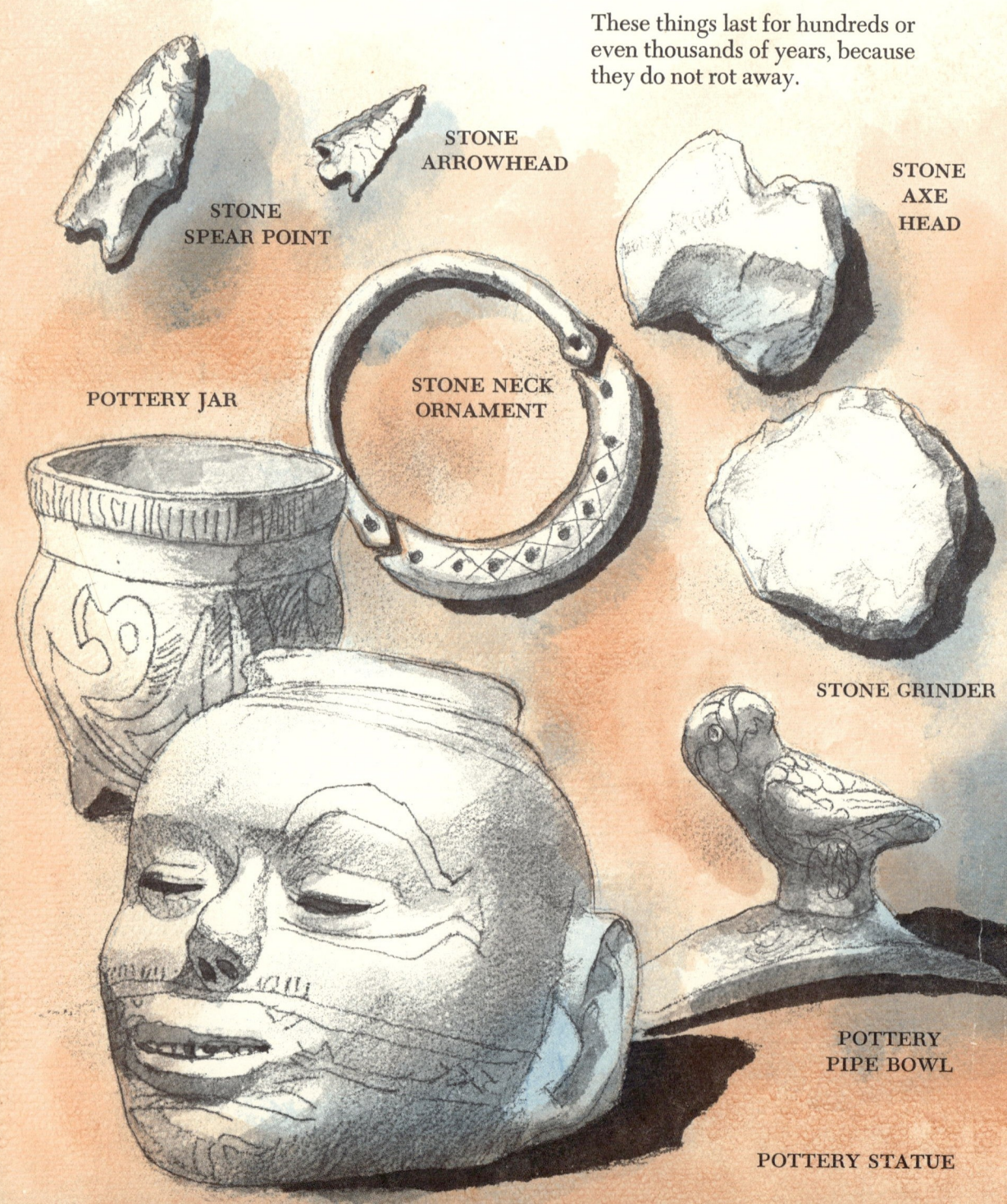

STONE SPEAR POINT

STONE ARROWHEAD

STONE AXE HEAD

POTTERY JAR

STONE NECK ORNAMENT

STONE GRINDER

POTTERY PIPE BOWL

POTTERY STATUE

Archaeologists find mostly those hard things that do not rot—such as tools made of stone or objects made of pottery. Sometimes bones and shells are found, but very seldom things made of cloth, leather, straw, or wood.

These ancient things are not often found by archaeologists. They usually rot away after a few hundred years.

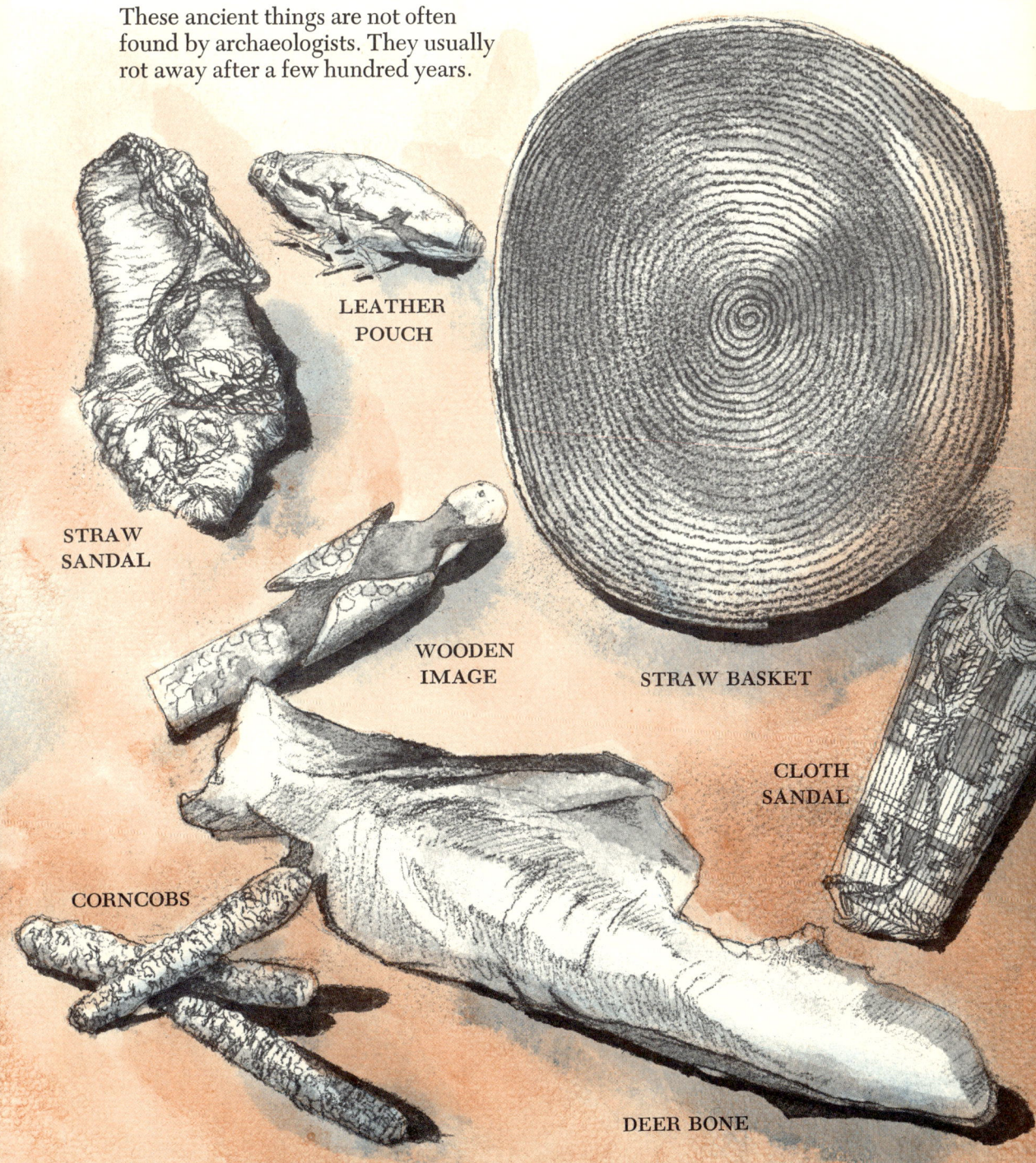

LEATHER POUCH

STRAW SANDAL

WOODEN IMAGE

STRAW BASKET

CLOTH SANDAL

CORNCOBS

DEER BONE

Archaeologists do not simply collect old
things. They study them, and try to
discover the way of life, or culture, of
the group of people that vanished long ago.

Culture includes the kinds of tools that
a group makes, their science and art, the
homes they made, and the clothes they wore.
Culture also includes their religion,
the way they got their food, and even the
way they acted toward each other and toward
people outside their group.

These are some of the things archaeologists
have learned about the cultures of people
who lived before the Indians:

Thick ice covered much of
the northern world 40,000 years ago,
as shown by the white areas.

Men may have first come to North America about 40,000 years ago, during the Ice Age. Men lived in Asia then, but there were no people in North America.

SIBERIA

ALASKA

The seas were shallower during the Ice Age. A "bridge" of land joined Asia and North America. People with a simple hunting culture traveled from Siberia to North America. We might call them the Ancient Hunters.

Ancient stone tool from British Mountain, Yukon, Canada

No human bones from the time of the Ancient Hunters have been found. But archaeologists have discovered some chipped-stone tools, and some beds of charcoal that may have been cooking places.

Many groups of Ancient Hunters followed animals from place to place. They traveled slowly southward, through a part of North America that was free of ice. As years went by, they learned to make better tools of stone—and probably of wood and bone as well.

Traces of very early man
have been found at various places
in both North America and South America.

The Ice Age ended about 11,000 years
ago, and the sea rose to cover the land
bridge to Asia. But by this time there
were probably many thousands of people
living in both North America and South America.

Spear point found with mammoth bones, southern Arizona

The people of 11,000 years ago had developed a new culture. They had learned to make very sharp chipped-stone points and fasten them to spears. With these weapons they could kill large animals such as bison, camels, and even mammoths. These people have been called the Big Game Hunters.

Folsom-type spear point, northeastern Colorado, about 10,000 years old

Point from Agate Basin, Wyoming, about 9,000 years old →

Point from Bull Brook, Massachusetts, about 8,000 years old

The chipped-stone points of the Big Game Hunters are found all over North and South America, but we really know very little about these people. Most of the things that were a part of their culture have disappeared. Even the bones of the people themselves have vanished, so we can only guess at what they looked like.

Life in the deserts of
western Utah about 7,000 years ago

Several thousand years passed. Separated
groups of people developed new cultures.
In warm, dry parts of the Southwest and West, the
Old Desert Culture people invented baskets.

The Old Desert Culture people hunted small animals and birds. They also gathered plant food such as grass seeds, acorns, roots, and berries. They invented stone grinders that turned the seeds to flour. Archaeologists have found the old grinders, baskets, and cords buried in dry western sands.

In places where forests grew, the
Big Game Hunting Culture changed into
another kind. The people learned to fish and
also to gather many kinds of shellfish
and plants. By about 9,000 years ago,
people in eastern North America learned to
make tools of polished stone as well as
chipped stone. They boiled water
by dropping hot stones into it.

People lived like this in southern Illinois from about 9,000 years ago until about 3,000 years ago.

Archaeologists call the culture of these people Archaic, a word meaning "old." The Archaic people made much better tools than the ancient Big Game Hunters. They had spear-throwers, swinging bolas to entangle animals, and woodworking tools. They invented the dugout canoe.

About 4,000 years ago, Archaic men made objects out of copper, which they found on Isle Royale in Lake Superior. They traded copper objects all over the Midwest.

The Archaic Culture in eastern North America lasted from about 9,000 years ago until about 3,000 years ago. During this time, man slowly learned how to live a better, easier life. Useful inventions were passed from place to place. Some groups of people learned much faster than others, and there were different kinds of Archaic Culture in different places.

People in middle Arizona and New Mexico lived in pit-houses 3,000 years ago and grew corn and squash.

The Archaic Culture and the Old Desert Culture did not end suddenly. Archaeologists usually say that a group of people passed out of these cultures when they learned to make pottery and plant corn. Corn came from Central America to the Southwest about 4,000 years ago. It did not reach eastern North America until later.

In Illinois, Burial Mound or Early Woodland people lived like this from about 4,000 years ago until about 2,500 years ago.

The culture that followed the Archaic in eastern North America is often called the Burial Mound Culture. About 3,000 years ago, some groups of people began to grow corn and live in large villages. They made pottery and built square houses.

These people developed a religion. Important people were buried in large mounds of earth together with pottery, jewelry, and other objects. The Burial Mound Culture spread into many parts of eastern North America. And as years went by, the mounds became larger and larger.

The Burial Mound Culture of southern Ohio, also called the Hopewell Culture

By about 500 B.C., the Mound Builders had learned to make beautiful pottery and handsome objects made of carved stone. They traded with faraway people to obtain copper and other materials for making jewelry. Today, archaeologists find all these things buried in the mounds together with the skeletons of important villagers.

The Burial Mound Culture came to an end about the year 500. In some places the people began to make very large mounds with temples on top but without any burials. In other places the people made hills shaped like birds, snakes, or other things. You can visit many of these mounds today.

In 1564, French colonists tried to settle in northern Florida among the Timucua Indians.

The first European explorers found a few Temple Mound tribes still living in eastern North America. In other places the people lived in villages, hunting and growing crops. Their culture is called Woodland. The explorers called the Eastern Woodland people "Indians."

This ancient Anasazi dwelling is now part of Canyon De Chelly National Monument, Arizona.

At the same time that some eastern people were building burial mounds, some groups in the Southwest were learning to make pottery and to form large communities. The "apartment house" dwellings we call pueblos were invented by the Anasazi people about 1,000 years ago.

Praying for rain.

Pueblo Bonito in New Mexico was a fortress village. By the year 1300 its people were gone.

For about 300 years the Anasazi and other town-dwelling southwestern people farmed and prospered. And then they vanished. Archaeologists do not know why. Perhaps enemy tribes or a lack of rainfall destroyed their culture.

People in ancient California had a culture similar to the Archaic Culture of the East. It changed little throughout the 2,000 years before the explorers came.

In some other parts of western North America, people lived more simple lives. In warm California the tribes were very small. They did not work much with pottery, nor did they grow many crops. Their culture stayed much the same for thousands of years as they hunted and gathered wild food.

Basket-making tribes of the Great Basin deserts have kept much the same culture for the past 8,000 years.

In the dry Great Basin, life was very hard. The people kept a culture much like the Old Desert Culture right up until the time that European settlers arrived.

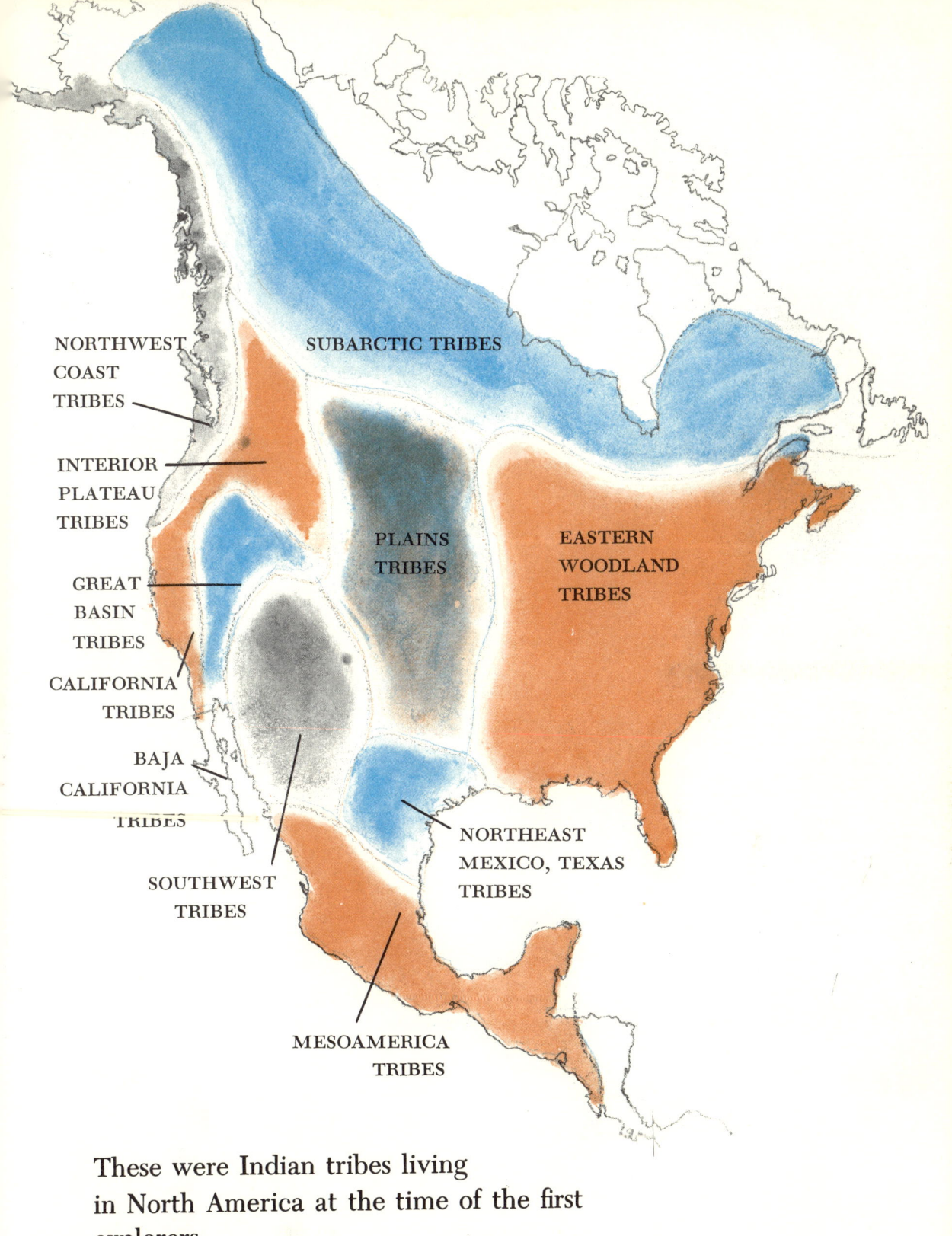

These were Indian tribes living in North America at the time of the first explorers.

The culture of the Chipewyan hunters and other Northland Indians remained Archaic.

In the cold forests of middle Canada, life was also very hard. The great glaciers lingered in the North long after they had melted in the South. The people who lived in middle Canada were hunters—and stayed hunters. They followed their food animals. Some of these groups moved southward to warmer lands and stayed there.

Much of the Eskimos' food comes from the sea.

Most archaeologists believe that the Eskimo people were the last to come to North America from Asia. Perhaps they came about 5,000 years ago. Their culture probably changed very little throughout this time. Eskimos are not Indians. They do not resemble Indians in their body form, nor are their language and culture like that of northern Indians.

Why did cultures change quickly in some places and stay the same for thousands of years in other places? Part of the answer lies in climate. If a climate is too harsh—as in the Northland or Great Basin desert—people must work hard just to stay alive.

But if the climate is too gentle
and if food can be found
without much effort, people get lazy. They
hardly ever think up new ideas. They feel
there is no need to change the old ways.
People seem to make progress—to learn, to
invent, and to live better—when life is
neither too hard nor too easy.

AUTHOR'S NOTE

Archaeologists and ethnologists differ somewhat in their interpretation of ancient cultures in North America. The principal authorities for the data in this book are Gordon R. Willey, *An Introduction to American Archaeology,* and J. D. Jennings and Edward Norbeck, *Prehistoric Man in the New World.*

There are many gaps and uncertainties in scientists' knowledge of early man in America. The text of this book reflects some of what is known or is highly probable but does not make a point of attempting to fill in unknown areas with speculation.